MONICA
'DEAREST BUN ...'

DENNIS TELFORD

First published in 2014
On behalf of Haydon Parish Council

This second edition published 2015

Copyright 2014/15 : Dennis Telford and those whose works and photographs have been used / quoted in the publication.
(See page i and ii)

Printed by Blake Printers Ltd., Haltwhistle, Northumberland.

ISBN : 978-0-9576531-5-3

TYNE VIEW
tyneviewpublishing@gmail.com

CONTENTS

Thank You
In the preparation of this 2014 edition
my thanks for advice and proof reading are due to:
James Booth : Don Lee
Mike Parkin : Richard Snowdon

**DEDICATED TO
THE PEOPLE
OF
THE PARISH OF HAYDON**

This work is an abridged version of an article first published in
The Haydon News, issues numbers 3-7, 2003; and an edited
version, with additional material, of a subsequent article
published in *Northern Review Volume 13, 2003-04.*

The Author

Dennis Telford was born in 1941 and has lived in Haydon Bridge
all his life. Now retired, he cultivates a keen interest in the
history of the Parish of Haydon.

BOOKS WRITTEN BY THE AUTHOR

WELCOME TO HAYDON BRIDGE
The Birthplace of John Martin

HAYDON OLD CHURCH
A Short History and Guide

MONICA : 'DEAREST BUN ...'

COOMBES' HISTORY OF LANGLEY BARONY
Edited with new material
(A Series)

SOURCES OF REFERENCE
and
ACKNOWLEDGEMENTS

Andrew Motion: *Philip Larkin - A Writer's Life,*
Published by Faber & Faber, 1993

I have followed Andrew Motion's account of events as
recorded in his biography of Philip. The Haydon Bridge
memories found within are substantially those from Monica
herself. Whether the biographical content is subscribed to
completely by the other women in Larkin's life is open to
question. Did Monica's account treat the other women
fairly?

Andrew Motion: *Breaking In*
Published in GRANTA Magazine No.41 1992

Andrew Motion's account of his visit to 1A, Ratcliffe Road
in 1989, to recover Larkin's letters to Monica, has been
invaluable. (*Breaking In* is in Appendix 2 on page 59)

Philip Larkin *Collected Poems*,
Faber and Faber, 1988, revised and published in paperback
in 1990 and 2003.

Anthony Thwaite (Ed.) *Selected Letters of Philip Larkin -
1940 to 1985* (Pub 1992) and *Philip Larkin Letters to
Monica* (Pub 2010) Both published by Faber and Faber.

The Philip Larkin Society Newsletter, *'About Larkin'* is a
must for anyone interested in Philip's work and life. If your
interest is purely related to Monica, I recommend issues
No.7 April 1999, No.11 April 2001 and No.12 October
2001.

The Society website is: http://www.philiplarkin.com

'Lucky Jim' was written by Kingsley Amis; first published
in Great Britain by Gollancz 1954. For my research, I have
used the Penguin Books 1961 edition, reprinted with an
introduction in 1992.

My thanks are due to The Society of Authors, the Literary Representative of the Estate of Philip Larkin, and Faber and Faber Ltd., for allowing me to use photographs and extracts from work by Andrew Motion, Anthony Thwaite and Philip Larkin.

There are many individuals whose published works, support and / or memories of Monica and Philip have inspired, and provided quotes and photographs for this work. I thank them all, but especially:

James Booth and Don Lee of the Philip Larkin Society for their support, advice and photographs.
Andrew Motion, for his good wishes and allowing me to publish *Breaking In*.
James Booth - *About Larkin* No's.7 1999: 11 2001: 12 2001.
Roger Craik - *About Larkin* No.11 2001.
John Ellis - *About Larkin* No.11 2001.
Donald W. Lee - *About Larkin* No.7 1999.
Prof. J.R. Watson - *About Larkin* No.11 2001 and Monica at Haydon Bridge (photographs).
Jean Humphreys - *About Larkin* No.12 2001 (photograph).
Hull History Centre - Cover photograph of Philip Larkin.
Alan Myers 1933-2010 - a champion of the literary heritage in the North East of England - and Bill Lancaster. Both Alan and Bill encouraged me to share my research with a wider audience.

Thanks are also due to the people of Haydon Bridge who remembered Monica and Philip and have expressed a view.

Monica's main friends and support at Haydon Bridge were her neighbours at number 3, and June Willis has given me an insight into Miss Jones' time in 1A which I couldn't have gained from previously published material. Thank you June.

As far as I am aware, Willie Mycock's purchase of 1A from Monica has never been part of the official Larkin / Monica Jones story. Thanks to Willie … It is now!

INTRODUCTION

'I thought your little house seemed … distinguished and exciting and beautiful: *you* have a great English river drifting under your window, brown and muscled with currents!' *(Philip Larkin - letter to Monica)*

'Its chief delight was a little yard at the back, which gave onto the river South Tyne, with the bridge in the centre of the view.' *(J.R. Watson - a colleague and friend of Monica's)*

"There weren't many other cars as smart as Philip's parked on Ratcliffe Road in those days!" *(Tony Willis - Monica's young neighbour)*

Back now to private addresses, gates and lamps
In high stone one-street villages, empty at dusk,
And side roads of small towns (sports final stuck
In front doors, allotments reaching down to the railway);
(Philip Larkin - Show Saturday)

'On Boxing Day morning … the Haydon Bridge Silver Band would go round the village playing. [Monica] got them to play 'Lead Kindly Light' which made Philip cry.' *(J.R. Watson - a colleague and friend of Monica's)*

"How is my little house?" "How is my river, is it high?" *(Monica - on the phone from Hull)*

"The weather forecasts are rather alarming, has there been frost, are my water pipes alright?" *(Monica - on the phone from Hull)*

'DEAREST BUN'

Philip Larkin was one of the greatest poets of the twentieth century, with an international reputation and a complicated private life, and yet few people knew that for twenty three years he spent some of his happiest times in Haydon Bridge.

In 1961, Philip Larkin's muse and lover, **Monica Jones,** bought **1A, Ratcliffe Road** in **Haydon Bridge** as a weekend and holiday cottage and it became a secret retreat for the couple. Initially sceptical, Philip fell in love with Monica's cottage where they were allowed to share an intimate relationship without interference, in a community where their fame went largely unnoticed.

1A, Ratcliffe Road was an unpretentious 'burrow' and Monica was Philip's 'Dearest Bun'.

Monica left Haydon Bridge for good, but with great sadness, in 1984 due to ill health, and went to live with Philip at his home in Hull where they were together until Philip's death in 1985.
Following Philip's death, Monica lived in deep sorrow, becoming an almost total recluse before her own death on February 15th 2001.

The memory of Miss Jones - as she was known by village people - and Philip Larkin to whom she was devoted, lives on in Haydon Bridge where a plaque adorns 1A, Ratcliffe Road, a cottage once described by Monica as her 'Piece of Heaven'; and this book is an introduction to their true life Haydon Bridge love story and the related events following Larkin's death.

Dennis Telford
2014

"Would he look after it?" "Would he love 1A?"
(Monica - asks about a prospective purchaser)

"She talked about Haydon Bridge as if it was Paradise ... She clearly loved it dearly." *(Willie Mycock - who bought 1A from Miss Jones)*

'The house was even smaller than I'd expected, and uglier. Packed into a tight row near the Old Bridge.' *(Andrew Motion - when he visited in 1989)*

'Those stairs are a menace. I have to come down them like a pregnant giraffe.' *(Philip - in a letter to Monica who had fallen on the stairs at 1A)*

'Philip's visits to Monica were during the formative period of his mature poems and Haydon Bridge must have had a significant influence.' *(Don Lee - The Philip Larkin Society)*

'She was buried on a fair February day, under the East Riding sky, in Cottingham cemetery.
I wondered if she and Philip would be buried side by side, but the graves have been spaced very regularly, so that she was a few rows away from him.' *(James Booth - The Philip Larkin Society)*

"Miss Jones was a special lady, well-educated and well spoken but equally at home when talking to the likes of us." *(June Willis - Monica's neighbour at Haydon Bridge)*

PHILIP, MONICA AND THEIR BURROW

In September 1946, when he was twenty-four, Philip Larkin went to work as sub-librarian at University College, Leicester. Within three weeks he had met Monica Jones, a lecturer in the English Department. After three years they had become lovers. After another six months Larkin left Leicester for the library at Queen's University, Belfast, where he stayed for five years, seeing Monica regularly but at widely-spaced intervals. In 1955 he was appointed Librarian at the University of Hull, and remained there for the last thirty years of his life.

During this time he and Monica took annual holidays together, met at least once a month, wrote to each other and/or spoke on the telephone nearly every day. The relationship was in certain respects deeply troubled (by jealousies, by distance), and in others very happy. Monica was Larkin's steadfast companion and his soul-mate. He dedicated *The Less Deceived* to her: it was the only collection of poems he dedicated to anyone.

In September 1961 Monica bought a small house in Haydon Bridge in Northumberland, on the main Newcastle-Carlisle road. (Her family had originally come from that part of the world.) She meant it to be a bolt-hole - somewhere she might escape the various worries of her private life and her university work. Larkin was initially suspicious of the house but soon admiring. He took holidays there, hunkered down in it for weekends, always visited at New Year. When he wouldn't or couldn't leave Hull, Monica was often in Haydon Bridge alone - writing Larkin letters, waiting for him to ring. The house was their special place, their burrow.

Andrew Motion
From 'Breaking In'
1992
(See Appendix 2)

There is still much work to do to determine the life Monica
and Philip led at Haydon Bridge; the places they visited
and the poems written in the cottage,
1A, Ratcliffe Road.

200 letters from Philip to Monica
were found at Haydon Bridge and
are available in the Brynmor Jones Library, Hull.
Monica's surviving letters to Philip are deposited
at the Bodleian Library, Oxford.

HAYDON BRIDGE
NORTHUMBERLAND

This love story and its associated research is centred around Monica Jones, her relationship with Philip Larkin and, especially, the Haydon Bridge connection.

**Haydon Bridge from the South East
with the
River South Tyne and the main Newcastle to Carlisle road
in the foreground.**

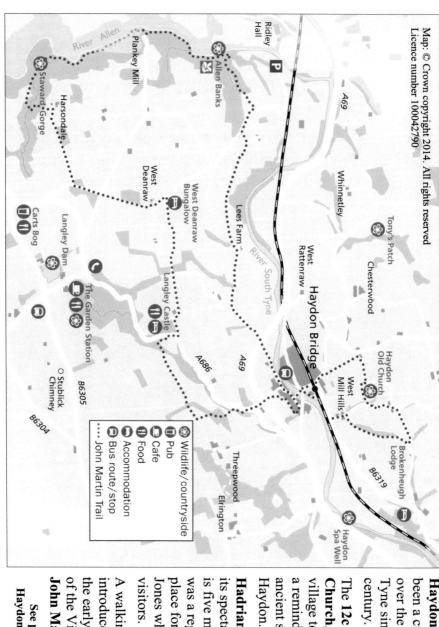

Map: © Crown copyright 2014. All rights reserved
Licence number 100042790

Legend:
- 🌼 Wildlife/countryside
- 🍺 Pub
- ☕ Cafe
- 🍴 Food
- 🛏 Accommodation
- 🚌 Bus route/stop
- ⋯ John Martin Trail

Haydon Bridge has been a crossing point over the River South Tyne since the 14th century.

The **12c Haydon Church**, above the village to the north, is a reminder of the ancient settlement of Haydon.

Hadrian's Wall and its spectacular scenery is five miles north and was a regular visiting place for Monica Jones when she had visitors.

A walking trail will introduce visitors to the early inspiration of the Victorian artist **John Martin**.

See page 65 for
Haydon Bridge detail

8

A BRIEF ENCOUNTER WITH HAYDON BRIDGE

Haydon Bridge lies comfortably between three suitors of outstanding natural beauty; flirting with the southern boundary of the Northumberland National Park, kissed by the extremes of the North Pennines Area of Outstanding Natural Beauty and forever a close companion of Hadrian's Wall. (A 'World Heritage Site') The village lies on the banks of the great River Tyne, courts the affection and shares the joy and pleasure of such close companions and yet is happy to maintain its independence.

And why not?

Haydon Bridge and its surrounding parish is itself a place of romance and legend and of extraordinary heritage and rare beauty, waiting to catch the eye and tempt any would be admirer to delight in its charms.

Stand on the bridge that gave my 14th century village its name and gaze **westwards** as the reflections from a bright sun and clear blue sky play on the 'singing waters' of the Tyne; or watch in awe as the dark clouds from Cumberland deposit their burden into the river thundering below you.
Look to the **east** where the salmon leap the waterfall in season and the majestic heron stalks its prey.
This is a river crossing that has endured the border raider, inspired the famous artist and stimulated the passionate poet.

To the **north,** our 12th century chapel of Haydon keeps a brooding and mysterious vigil over the remains of an ancient settlement, while above and to the **south,** Langley Castle stands tall and proud overlooking its mediaeval barony.

Haydon Bridge Station.   (photograph by John Irving)

Travelling by train on her frequent visits from Leicester, Monica Jones' first view of Haydon Bridge was the village railway station. Haydon Bridge is midway on the Newcastle and Carlisle cross country line.

In the early years, Monica arrived from the west from Leicester on the Thames Clyde Express via the Settle and Carlisle line, with a change at Carlisle for Haydon Bridge. After the long distance service via the Settle and Carlisle line was abandoned in 1976, Monica travelled from the east and her journey from Leicester required three changes, at Derby, York and Newcastle.

**Philip Larkin's '.. allotments reaching down to the railway .. '
at Haydon Bridge.**

Haydon Bridge from the south west.
1A, Ratcliffe Road is on the left at the north end of the bridge.

'You have a great English river drifting under your window'

Philip Larkin's view of the River South Tyne
from 1A, Ratcliffe Road, Haydon Bridge.

11

1A, Ratcliffe Road from the south east.
After Monica sold the cottage, a new kitchen was built across
this south elevation altering the character of the house.

The General Havelock Inn at Haydon Bridge,
from where Monica 'borrowed' Merlin the cat.
It was here where Philip met North East poet Basil Bunting.

MONICA
'DEAREST BUN ...'

A HAYDON BRIDGE LOVE STORY

CHAPTER I

MISS JONES

When Andrew Motion knocked on the door of number 3 Ratcliffe Road, Haydon Bridge in 1989 and asked for the keys of number 1A, the property next door, the occupier June Willis was understandably cautious.

"What is it that you want in Miss Jones' cottage?"

"I'm hoping to find some of Monica's letters. I am writing a book about Philip Larkin". Motion replied.

"A book about Philip!! What has _he_ done that is worth writing about?"

I suspect that in spite of Philip Larkin's reputation as one of the finest poets of our time, most people in my village of Haydon Bridge would have been similarly surprised. The literary love nest that was **1A, Ratcliffe Road** was a well kept secret for over twenty three years, as the owner Monica Jones and her constant companion Philip Larkin lived out their intimate relationship there.

Few residents knew Miss Jones, the occupier of the stone-built terraced cottage opposite the village Post Office, and her significance in the life of one of the greatest poets of the 20th century. Of course she had neighbours, had her post delivered, her windows cleaned, general house repairs carried out and visited our village shops for her essential purchases, but maybe it wasn't until she left the property in 1984 and a number of inquisitive visitors turned up on her doorstep, and in poet and biographer Andrew Motion's case, retrieved unopened correspondence from behind the door opening onto Ratcliffe Road, that the rest of us suddenly sat up and began to take notice.

CHAPTER II

PHILIP AND ...

To fully understand the story of Monica and Philip and their connection with Haydon Bridge, it is necessary to consider some background information; to reflect on Philip Larkin's character and to dip in and out of his other relationships.

Philip Larkin was born in Coventry on 9th August 1922 to Eva and Sydney - parents, and a subsequent family life he strongly resents in his writing. For example in 1946 he wrote:

'Let me remember that the only married state I intimately know (i.e. that of my parents) is bloody hell.'

His upbringing had a significant influence on his own lifelong attitude that:

'Human beings should not live together' and that 'children should be taken from their parents at an early age.'

And yet, Eva his 'awful whining mother' had a major part to play in shaping his poems, life and relationships. Her demands on his time and his regular visits to see her as a dutiful son until her death on 17th November 1977 aged 91, gave him a reason to maintain the independence he craved, while at the same time entering into a series of relationships with other women, often simultaneously.

After graduating from Oxford with a First Class Honours Degree in English, Larkin became a librarian in Wellington, Shropshire in 1943 where he met Ruth Bowman. On her eighteenth birthday they became lovers and were eventually engaged to be married.

Monica Jones was born on 7th May 1922 an only child. Her father Frederick was Welsh and her mother was Margaret Lily (nee Peart) from St John's Chapel near Stanhope. It was this North East connection to which Monica's move to Haydon Bridge in 1961 has been attributed. Monica read English at Oxford and in 1943 she applied for a job at Leicester University where she remained throughout her career. In 1946 Philip Larkin was appointed Assistant Librarian at the University College of Leicester and it was here that Monica entered his life.

By 1950, Larkin's intense and hectic seven year relationship with Ruth Bowman was ending, while his three year friendship with Monica Jones was becoming more intimate.

In October 1950 Philip Larkin moved to Queen's University Belfast as Sub-Librarian; an escape perhaps from his engagement to Ruth, his affair with Monica and the increasing demands on his life by his mother Eva, with whom he had lived since his father's death in 1948.

Larkin's life became more complicated as new relationships developed in Belfast - a flirtatious friendship with Winifred Arnott, a graduate working in the library, and a promiscuous liaison with a friend's wife, Patsy Strang.

Monica's selfless commitment to their relationship, however, surmounted any problems Larkin's affairs may have caused. They continued to meet regularly in Belfast and Leicester and go on holiday together. Theirs was a friendship described by Larkin as, 'intimate and undemanding'. Monica was not intruding upon his independence!

In March 1955 Philip Larkin took up the position of Librarian at the University of Hull and in the same year a collection of his work, *The Less Deceived,* was published. It was dedicated to: 'Miss Monica Jones'.
This wasn't Larkin's first publication but it established his reputation as one of the foremost poets of the 20th century.

Apart from Eva, his mother, with whom he had a love-hate relationship, Larkin's main companion away from his work and literary friends was Monica who lived in Leicester. Monica Jones is described as suiting Philip Larkin as, 'their affair was always conducted at a distance, she was full of fun. ... And she was willing to go to bed with him whenever he wanted'. They both accepted that they were best off as they had always been, 'loving but unmarried'. I assume that this satisfied Larkin particularly, given his determination to live alone without threat to his independence.

Late in 1959 Monica Jones's mother and father died within two months of each other. The cosy relationship Larkin was enjoying was at once threatened. Monica's singular love for him meant that she had few other friends.
Without her parents would she become more reliant on him? Would she want to move into his Hull home with him? She might even approach the subject which they had discussed quite seriously in several letters, but to which he couldn't reconcile himself - marriage!!

When Monica needed her lover most, Philip Larkin in his despair at what the future might hold with her, turned to a member of his staff at Hull University, Maeve Brennan, for succour. Larkin and Maeve had worked together for five years but in early 1960 he encouraged a more personal relationship. A defence against Monica's sense of being, 'so alone'. A new threat to his independent lifestyle.
Was Philip Larkin unfairly selfish for much of his life or did he truly believe that marriage and domesticity would have been detrimental to his writing?
Maeve Brennan was of a strong Catholic faith and her principles determined that she would not enter into a sexual relationship outside marriage. Her close friendship with Larkin is described as, 'sensual but not intimate'.

Philip Larkin was now dealing with the anxiety caused by three very different relationships - the two lovers in his life, Monica Jones and Maeve Brennan and his responsibilities to his widowed mother.

Monica had been in this situation before of course, only this time, her spirits low following the death of her parents, she tried hard to make a change. When she discovered Larkin's

17

feelings for Maeve, feelings emphasised by hundreds of letters sent between them, she was particularly depressed and determined to have a house of her own, far away from Hull and Leicester, where she would try to live a life less dependent on Larkin. Or perhaps she was testing Larkin and his love for her against his other relationships. Monica was determined to find out where she stood in Philip Larkin's life.

CHAPTER III

A LITERARY LOVE NEST

Monica was drawn to the North East where her mother Margaret had lived.
In August 1961 she bought 1A, Ratcliffe Road in Haydon Bridge, where she would live at weekends and during her University vacations.

Philip Larkin's biographer, Andrew Motion, describes the small house in Haydon Bridge.

1A, Ratcliffe Road

'Two up and two down, white painted, simple, on the main Newcastle to Carlisle road, it looked nothing at all from the front. At the back (Monica) discovered a kind of miracle: the River Tyne, seventy five yards across at this point inland, rushing a few feet beyond the kitchen window - placid and muttering in summer, swollen and angry in winter, crashing branches against the old stone bridge which stands a short distance down stream. Monica wanted the house because of this view, because Haydon Bridge was an excellent starting point for holidays and sight-seeing in the north of England, and because having a place of her own made her less dependent on Larkin.'

Philip Larkin wasn't impressed by Monica's move to become less dependent upon him. Haydon Bridge is over 150 miles from where he lived in Hull, and Larkin didn't drive a car when Monica first bought the property.
A journey by public transport via Selby or York and Newcastle was not one that he would have looked forward to. It is very likely that Larkin's first thoughts about our village in the 'Far North' would have advanced his natural tendency to gloom and depression. Not for long however. As soon as Philip Larkin visited Monica for the first time,

19

he changed his mind about her house and soon began to appreciate its Haydon Bridge location.

On April 11th 1962, Larkin wrote to Monica:

'I thought your little house seemed … distinguished and exciting and beautiful: clever of you to have found it, bold of you to have furnished it in Rabbit Regency: it looks splendid, and it can never be ordinary with the Tyne going by outside. Others may have Swedish glass, or Swedish forks, or Finnish clap-boarding, or theatre in the round round the corner, or a Picasso, or a stereo hi-fi, or a split-level living area - *you* have a great English river drifting under your window, brown and muscled with currents!'

When Monica bought the property this view could be seen from the living room. After she sold the cottage, a new kitchen was built across the south elevation, replacing the old lean-to affair, and the character of the house was altered.

Monica had persuaded Larkin to visit her in 1962. She needed him in spite of her show of dependency and the fact that he had hurt her. Philip Larkin also needed Monica in spite of his new 'innocent' love Maeve Brennan, and after all Haydon Bridge could turn out to be, 'An exciting escape away from the world they both knew …' There would be few restrictions to whatever life they chose to lead in 1A, Ratcliffe Road.

Andrew Motion, Philip Larkin's biographer, tells his readers that Philip and Monica: 'lazed, drank, read, pottered around the village and amused themselves with private games.' 'Private games', I fancy, that would have shocked the elderly ladies of Haydon Bridge as they wandered past the front door of 1A going about their daily business.

In May 1962 Monica celebrated her 40th birthday, as did Larkin in August of the same year. Their relationship was recovering from the trauma of early 1961, but away from Haydon Bridge Larkin's attraction to Maeve Brennan was just as strong.

20

Monica's life with Philip Larkin was soon back on familiar ground. A mix of secrecy and lies, hurt and happiness, apologies and passion.

This emotional love affair continued in varying intensity until 1978 when, according to Motion, Maeve accepted that if anyone was likely to become Larkin's regular companion it would be Monica Jones.

Throughout the ups and downs of their relationship, it appears that Philip's visits to the Tyne Valley to be with Monica, invariably cheered them both up.

Larkin's biographer tells us that when Philip drove up to Haydon Bridge from Hull: 'As always the place worked its spell.'

Larkin would commit himself to Monica, Monica had him to herself and they spent many happy hours together in their 'Secret Hideaway' far from the complication of their real world. Monica and Philip lazed away their time together in the terraced cottage on Ratcliffe Road and also used it as a starting point for visits into Scotland, to Skye, to the Lake District and, locally, Hadrian's Wall and occasional nights at the Lord Crewe Arms in Blanchland - a favourite retreat.

It is unlikely that anyone in Haydon Bridge knew Monica and Philip better than their neighbours on Ratcliffe Road, the Willis' family.

A young Tony Willis was understandably impressed by Philip's car.

When Larkin passed his driving test in 1963 he bought a Singer Gazelle Automatic, principally so that he could take Maeve Brennan to places that she wanted to visit, but it also allowed him to visit Haydon Bridge much more easily than using public transport.

Tony's memories are more likely to have been of Larkin's next car however, a Vanden Plas Princess he bought in 1969 for his 47th birthday. Tony told me:

"There weren't many other cars as smart as Philip's parked on Ratcliffe Road in those days!"

In 1964 a collection of thirty-two of Philip Larkin's poems, *The Whitsun Weddings* was published by Faber & Faber to wide acclaim; in 1965 he received the Queen's Gold Medal for poetry.

Philip Larkin was basically a shy man and shunned public appearances, reviews, readings of his poems and the like. He was dubbed, 'the Hermit of Hull.' In 1966 however he was the subject of a BBC 'Monitor' programme.
Andrew Motion, in his biography, describes Philip on the programme as, 'a bald, slim, bespectacled man in the three-quarter length pale fawn Macintosh, nervously swallowing his stammer.'

Philip was much more at ease in Haydon Bridge.

To Werner Nagel, our village newsagent, Larkin was, "a nice man. At first glance a most unlikely womaniser: in his rimmed glasses he epitomised an absent-minded professor when visiting the shop with Monica to buy the *Observer* and *Telegraph*." Maybe Philip was about to read his own jazz column, another of his loves, which he started writing in 1961. In 1970 a compilation of his *Telegraph* reviews was published by Faber, '*All What Jazz: A Record Diary 1961 - 1971.*'

In 1970 and 1971 Monica's relationship with Larkin was as comfortable as it had been for some time and for New Year's Eve 1971 he drove up to Haydon Bridge and the two of them went to the New Year celebration at Allendale as usual, for the, 'Big Town Bonfire, the band and Old Lang Syne' where, 'the men of the village walk in a procession carrying tubs of blazing pitch on their heads.' Philip described the scene in a letter to Eva, his mother.

Another event in our locality that Monica and Philip Larkin visited on a number of occasions was the Bellingham Show. In 1973, after calling in at the show following a holiday in Scotland, Larkin wrote his poem, '*Show Saturday*' describing the scene which to him represented 'Old England' through its ancient pleasures and customs:
22

…..a man with pound notes round his hat… a tent selling
Tweed… folks sit about on bales… two young men in
acrobats' tights… four brown eggs, four white eggs, four
plain scones, four dropped scones…

*Philip reflects on a return (to Haydon Bridge) as the show
closes:*

For far-off farms. The pound note man decamps.
The car park has thinned. They're loading jumps on a truck.
Back now to private addresses, gates and lamps
In high stone one-street villages, empty at dusk,
And side roads of small towns (sports final stuck
In front doors, allotments reaching down to the railway);
Back now to autumn, leaving the ended husk
Of summer that brought them here for Show Saturday -

*And his poem ends in hope that the time honoured tradition
will:* '… always be there.'

Perhaps '*Show Saturday*' was composed overlooking the
South Tyne in the south-facing first floor bedroom in 1A,
Ratcliffe Road where, June Willis told me, Philip spent a lot
of time writing when he stayed with Monica. John Ellis, a
lecturing colleague and friend of Monica's recounts a story
she told him. 'Philip had looked broody after their visit to
the Bellingham Show, so she knew a poem was on its way.'

'*Show Saturday*' is included in the last collection of
Larkin's poems published during his lifetime, *High
Windows* published by Faber & Faber in 1974. Almost
20,000 copies were sold in the first year enhancing Philip
Larkin's already formidable poetic reputation.

In November 1975 Monica accompanied Philip to
Buckingham Palace where he received the CBE from the
Queen.
"I suppose I'll have to go and mix with the nobs," Monica
told June, who is sure that if it hadn't been that she was
accompanying Philip, Monica would have preferred to be in
Haydon Bridge.

Monica Jones was by now at Larkin's side during most of his public engagements and his visits to her Haydon Bridge hideaway continued.

Philip wasn't prepared to commit himself completely to Monica however. Maeve Brennan still shared his life, as did Betty Mackereth, his secretary since 1957, with whom there seems to have been no previous romantic involvement, until a secret affair between the two of them started in 1975. Larkin also continued to visit his mother Eva regularly, until her death in 1977.

In 1978 Larkin and Maeve split romantically although they still worked together. Monica was Philip's regular companion now and although she knew about his other intimate relationship with his secretary, she apparently accepted it without too much fuss.

In 1982, 60 year old Monica retired from her lecturing position at Leicester University. She planned to spend more time at Haydon Bridge. To Philip Larkin, Monica was his, 'Bun' or 'Bunny', a reference to Beatrix Potter's stories. In this affectionate context Monica's Ratcliffe Road home was known to them both as her 'Rabbit Hole'.

Next door, the young Tony and Jacqueline Willis had their own pet bunnies. June Willis recalled that Monica loved their rabbits, her favourite animal, and she would often ask to see them. On one occasion Philip knocked on the door and asked if he could take a photograph of Monica with Tony and Jacqueline's pets and the shot was taken in the small back yard overlooking the river South Tyne.

Monica had never learned to drive and unless visiting 1A accompanied by Philip, she had to make a none too easy journey from Leicester to Carlisle via the Settle - Carlisle line, and then on to Haydon Bridge; an indication of how much she enjoyed her time in the village.

Professor J.R. Watson was a colleague and friend of Monica's at Leicester. He describes the house at Haydon Bridge as being, 'tiny, in a short terrace on the main road:

24

its chief delight was a little yard at the back, which gave onto the river South Tyne, with the bridge in the centre of the view.'

Professor Watson recounts a particularly moving moment as told to him by Monica.

'On Boxing Day morning ... the Haydon Bridge Silver Band would go round the village playing. She (Monica) got them to play 'Lead Kindly Light' which made Philip cry.'

In October 1982 alone at Haydon Bridge, Monica fell down the stairs and was taken to Hexham Hospital where she had 'umpteen' stitches in a head wound. Larkin drove up from Hull and took her back with him to convalesce. From this time Monica appears to have had doubts about being able to live on her own. At the end of November, however, they returned to Ratcliffe Road in the hope that she could manage herself.

Worse was to follow. Perhaps best described by Philip Larkin himself in a letter to Anthony Thwaite who was to become his Literary Executor.

'... I am writing from Haydon Bridge (9th April 1983) ... this is the end of what had been a ghastly week. Monica and I came up on Good Friday, really to see that the cottage had survived the winter and perhaps for Monica to look at houses. She was not feeling well and was worse on Saturday with pains in the head and neck. On Sunday these were so intense that I rang the local GP, who to his eternal credit came the same morning and diagnosed shingles ... it is an awful business, swelling of the face and left eye till it closed completely, and great feeling of lowness... Tuesday Monica plummeted and was so silent and unresponsive I felt very unhappy about it all, even though doctor or nurse came daily... the Haydon Bridge doctor is clearly worried about Monica's general state, and so am I... At the risk of sounding self-centred I can add I've felt awful too. Worried, of course, and distressed at her state, but also trapped and terrified when it seemed we should be here indefinitely ... Even the cottage, which is very small, made me claustrophobic. Three nights I spent in an armchair drinking and smoking and dozing... I have been isolated up here, though the doctor and nurses have been very good. I do hope I can get Monica up and off.'

Within a day or two Monica and Philip closed up the house on Ratcliffe Road and returned to Hull where Monica could attend the Royal Infirmary.

It was a year before Monica had recovered sufficiently to make an attempt to look after herself again and in March 1984 Philip drove her up to Haydon Bridge where she stayed for a few 'freezing days'. Larkin described the cottage as, 'rather grim after a year's vacancy - spiders, and the telephone cut off.'

When he returned home alone, Philip realised how much he was missing Monica and he wrote to her on successive days, enquiring about her health and general situation. When the telephone was reconnected at 1A, Ratcliffe Road, Monica rang for Philip. He motored up to Haydon Bridge and they returned to Hull together.

This was to be the last visit to their Haydon Bridge 'Love Nest' which had served them so well for twenty-three years. A 'little house' that Monica adored and, in happier times, of which Andrew Motion wrote:

'... Larkin sank gratefully into obscurity ... and found once again that the place cheered him up.'

CHAPTER IV

THE PARTING

In early April 1984 following her illness, diagnosed by Dr. Robert High as shingles, Monica left Haydon Bridge for good to live with Philip at his home in 105, Newland Park, Hull. It was there where they spent the last months of their time together.

Larkin's health was now deteriorating. Throughout his life he had worried about 'the moment of (his) death' and now he had convinced himself that he was making 'steady progress to the grave.' Even though she wasn't in the best of health herself, Monica nursed Philip through his final illnesses.

The Philip Larkin story was not quite complete however!

On 19th May 1984, John Betjeman, the Poet Laureate, died and in December the Prime Minister, Margaret Thatcher, offered Larkin the position. Perhaps due to his natural shyness in public, his unwillingness to accept the media attention associated with the role or, in his own words,

' …the compulsion to write poems left me about seven years ago, since when I have written virtually nothing. Naturally this is a disappointment, but I would sooner write no poems than bad poems … I think the above circumstances disqualifies me for the Laureateship.'

Larkin declined the offer and Ted Hughes became Poet Laureate in succession to Betjeman. The offer had come too late for Philip.

Mrs Thatcher was nevertheless determined to honour him. His critical views on trade unionists, socialists, immigrants and anything foreign may well have appealed, and in June 1985 he was made a Companion of Honour.

Philip was too ill to attend Buckingham Palace to receive it.

27

Monica Jones 1947 photographed by Philip Larkin
Pub. 'About Larkin' April 2001. © the Estate of Philip Larkin

Monica Jones at Leicester 1976
Pub. 'About Larkin' October 2001. © Jean Humphreys

Monica (about 1975) in the back yard at
1A, Ratcliffe Road, Haydon Bridge.
Pub. 'About Larkin' April 2001.
(photograph provided by J.R. Watson)

Philip and Monica outside Buckingham Palace
Pub. 'A Writer's Life', 1993. © the Estate of Philip Larkin

Philip Larkin died aged 63 years in hospital at Hull on 2nd December 1985 of cancer of the oesophagus.

Monica was devastated by his death and too distraught to attend his funeral at the University Church of St. Mary the Virgin in Cottingham near Hull. Despite her deep sorrow and own illnesses, she attended a memorial service held at Westminster Abbey on the 14th February 1986.

Now Monica, who had given almost forty years to the man she loved, was alone. Andrew Motion describes her as, 'Isolated at (Larkin's home) Hull, ill and virtually unknown to the outside world ..... she had no existence without Larkin although she had all his possessions around her.'

Monica did have one final act to carry out on Philip's behalf, however: to destroy his personal diaries which he had kept assiduously throughout his life. She rang Betty Mackereth, Larkin's secretary and another of his lovers, to ask for her help and over thirty A4 notebooks of a great poet's intimate memories, some shared in the terraced house on Ratcliffe Road, were shredded and incinerated at his death-bed request - an unfortunate event for Larkin historians and literary sleuths, but a clear sign of Monica's undying love for, and commitment to, Philip.
We are not without record of Monica's and Philip's time in Tynedale, however. From 1968 they decided to keep a diary together. This was not part of the material destroyed.

Andrew Motion's fine biography, *Philip Larkin - A Writer's Life,* includes Monica's memories of the Haydon Bridge connection. Larkin's poems reflect the life he led, and further research, particularly of archived letters and photographs, may determine which of these are likely to have been written at Haydon Bridge. Don Lee, of the Philip Larkin Society, makes the point that Philip's visits to Monica were during the formative period of his mature poems and Haydon Bridge must have had a significant influence. Not least, we have the personal memories of those in our village who remember Monica and Philip.

After Philip's death Monica seldom left the house in Hull, becoming a total recluse in the final year of her own life and bed-ridden in her last months. She continued to enquire about the Ratcliffe Road property, however, although she was never well enough to return to it.

"How is my little house?" she would enquire of June Willis by phone.
"How is my river, is it high?"
"Have the storms in the north damaged my slates?"
"The weather forecasts are rather alarming, has there been frost, are my water pipes alright?"

June was usually able to allay Monica's concerns and put her mind at rest, but she felt, "really sorry for Monica, her voice was so weak on the phone".

It was no surprise to June that Monica's Haydon Bridge cottage was still dominating her thoughts. She had expressed great sadness when she locked the front door for the last time and Philip drove her away from the village in April 1984.

"I am afraid that it is most unlikely that I shall ever return to my little house."

105, Newland Park, Hull. Philip Larkin's home where Monica lived from leaving Haydon Bridge in April 1984 until her death on 15th February 2001. © James Booth

CHAPTER V

VISITORS

In 1986, Monica Jones, herself very ill and frail in Hull and
worrying about her house in Haydon Bridge, decided it was
time to authorise a story of Philip's life and she asked
Andrew Motion to write Larkin's biography.
Motion writes: 'Monica said nothing about the letters Larkin
had written her. If I asked where they were she would shrug
- lighting another cigarette, pouring another drink ... . One
day, out of the blue, she said most of the letters were in
Haydon Bridge.'

Monica was too ill to travel with Andrew Motion to retrieve
the letters, yet she didn't want anyone to visit the Ratcliffe
Road cottage unless she was with them. 'The house was
theirs: a secret place, where she and Larkin had lived to the
exclusion of all others ... . Once the door had been opened,
that life would be over.'
Eventually, in the autumn of 1989, Monica relented and he
drove to Haydon Bridge without her.

I'll let Andrew Motion take up the story. He opens with a
Northumberland climate stereotype we will all recognise,
but firmly dispute as the norm.

'We roller-coastered the wet road towards Hexham, then on.
Rain was swirling in from the North Sea behind us. So
much had fallen in recent weeks, the moors were yellow and
sour-looking. As we ducked down into Haydon Bridge,
streams bulged in the ditches beside us.

The house was even smaller than I'd expected, and uglier.
Packed into a tight row near the Old Bridge, on the main
road, it had a jaded white front, a slate roof, plain modern
windows and a front door which opened straight off the
street. I got the key from a neighbour and opened up ... the
rain falling on my neck and back ... I shoved the door
violently and we were in. A tiny box of a hall; the sitting

room to the left; stairs rising straight ahead. The stairs looked crazy.

Outside the window at the back beyond a cramped cement yard ... there flowed a gigantic river. The Tyne; ... I saw a full-grown tree sweep past, then heard the trunk grinding against the bridge away to my left, out of sight ... .

... Monica hadn't told me where I might find the letters, but it didn't matter. They were everywhere. In books, down the side of a chair, under a rug, on the window seat. A few lay flat and saturated in the yard ... .

It was the same upstairs .. I went into the lumber room, into a jungle of clothes and hangers which had a small box at its heart, stuffed with letters. ... In the smaller bedroom, under the window overlooking the river, a bed with letters both inside and underneath it. In the larger bedroom; more letters in books, an empty case of wine, an ironing board with a half -ironed dress draped across it.'

Andrew Motion pushed the letters into plastic bags, returned the key to June Willis, climbed into his car and left to return to Monica - and sunnier climes no doubt!

June was left to reflect on Andrew Motion's visit and the questions he had asked her. Until that day she hadn't been aware of the fame and attention her neighbours were about to attract.

"A book about Philip's life with Monica! I just couldn't believe it," June said to me.

Monica's house had been unoccupied for five and a half years and Andrew Motion was probably the only official visitor during that time. Sadly, in the twilight of Monica's ownership, the property was burgled - fortunately not a regular occurrence in my village although it was probably the third time that number 1A had been broken into.

After the first incident, Monica and Philip responded to June's phone call by driving up to Haydon Bridge to assess the damage. Monica was particularly concerned that a secret compartment in the floor of the wardrobe had not been opened. To her relief, personal effects hadn't been taken. The intruders had apparently been satisfied with bottles of wine and spirits. Arrangements were made for a village joiner to fit a bolt to an inner door to deter unwelcome visitors in the future.

It is interesting that neither Monica nor Philip thought it wise to remove the correspondence which contained the story of their relationship. The 'love' letters belonged in the secret place they had shared, 1A, Ratcliffe Road, whatever the consequences.

The second break-in was discovered by Andrew Motion on his visit. When he pushed open the door against a 'mound of junk mail on the mat' he was confronted by 'drawers in a sideboard lolled open, empty … books all over the floor, books flung about for the 'hell of it' and a broken window at the rear, a hole like a starburst and slivers of glass on the purple carpet.'

If those responsible should by any chance read this story, they may be interested to know that the real valuables, which they overlooked, were the letters from Philip to Monica strewn through every room.

The third burglary, which followed Andrew Motion's visit, was of a much more serious nature. The front door was kicked open, rooms were broken into and vases, china ornaments, silver and even items of furniture were stolen.

In June's words: "The whole house was turned upside down."

CHAPTER VI

SAD STEPS

When Monica's unoccupied cottage on Ratcliffe Road was broken into for the third time, Hexham Police recommended to Miss Jones that if she wasn't going to occupy the property again then she should consider selling it. A very sad Monica reluctantly agreed and asked her neighbour, June Willis, to arrange for the sale of the remaining furniture and seek an Estate Agent's valuation of Number 1A.

"I would thank you for keeping my name out of it," implored Monica. June respected her confidence.

Having agreed to part with her 'little house' which held so many memories of her life with Philip Larkin, Monica was eager to find a new owner who was from Haydon Bridge and would be sure to take good care of the property.
June recommended Willie Mycock, a village joiner who had recently started his West End Joinery business and would be a first-time buyer.

"Would he look after it?"
"Would he be able to improve it satisfactorily?"
"Would he love 1A?" As she had done.

After assurances from June, Monica gave permission for Willie to contact her at Hull.

Following a telephone call to Monica, Willie Mycock pulled his van up outside the front door of the cottage on Ratcliffe Road, got a key from June Willis and pushed open the door. The inside of the house was in a dreadful state, empty and neglected for six years, not to mention the chaos caused by unwelcome intruders.
A few sticks of furniture remained after the burglaries and house clearance. Willie loaded a sideboard, small tables, ornaments, boxes of odds and ends and some window drapes, specifically asked for by Monica, into his van as he

had promised "Miss Jones" he would, and set off on his journey to Humberside.

"Why she wanted those old drapes I'll never know," commented her neighbour June. Maybe of sentimental value?

When Willie Mycock arrived in Hull at 105 Newland Park, he made his way to the rear door. Monica had told him on the telephone that she would be unable to walk to the door but it would be left open and he should let himself in. When he approached the cul-de-sac that is Newland Park, the twenty-five year old joiner from Haydon Bridge was impressed. Brick built in the 1950s, it was: "A kind of posh area. A leafy suburb. Neat gardens. Quiet and yet ideally situated."
Once inside he wasn't quite so sure. Number 105 was the first house Larkin had owned and where he had lived his independent life from 1974 until his death. Monica had advised on Philip's original internal decoration and Willie's recollection of his visit is that little in the way of tidying up or maintenance had been done in the intervening sixteen years. "They weren't what you could call house proud," he told me.

Monica was alone in the house. In a chair in the green-walled sitting room, quite unable to get about - obviously a shadow of the vibrant lecturer at Leicester and the lady who had spent twenty-three years at Haydon Bridge.
The room was "crammed with pieces of furniture, (Larkin's) record collections and books galore", not placed neatly in the cabinets for effect but, "lying everywhere".
Number 105 Newland Park was for living in! These books were for reading!

Monica Jones suffered greatly from the trauma of Philip Larkin's death and the effects of her own debilitating illnesses; shingles and severe arthritis. The few people who saw her in her later years all remark on her worsening physical health and well-being. Surrounded by Philip's

36

furniture and mementoes, Monica sought comfort and perhaps eased the pain, from a glass. When Willie Mycock spoke to me about his visit, his first memory was of, "benches littered with empty spirit bottles".

Monica's mind and memory weren't affected and for two or three hours she talked to Willie about her time at Haydon Bridge, her frequent train journeys from Leicester, the feeling of nearing "home" once onto the Newcastle - Carlisle line; her house on Ratcliffe Road and the River Tyne sweeping past her yard at the rear; Langley Castle and Langley Dam; Hadrian's Wall; Allendale, Allenheads and many other places in the area she visited with Philip.

Monica shared her joy of our wonderful countryside with Willie. She showed him photographs and talked with enthusiasm about them. When I discussed the visit with Willie, his memory of the details was sketchy after twelve or thirteen years, but Monica's love for Haydon Bridge had left a lasting impression.

"She talked about Haydon Bridge as if it was Paradise," he told me. "I was thinking about the A69 running through the middle of the village; *(before it was by-passed)* constant traffic, noise and fumes. Miss Jones was describing a place I could hardly recognise. She clearly loved it dearly."

Monica's enthusiastic talk about Haydon Bridge and her time here had a downside. She began to change her mind about selling the property. Even though it was clearly impossible, she resurrected thoughts of a return someday. Eventually, after more reasoned thinking and gentle persuasion from the prospective purchaser, common sense prevailed. With a sadness in her heart Monica accepted Willie Mycock's offer of the £15,000 valuation.
He unloaded his van into the garage at Newland Park and made his return to the stone-built riverside terraced cottage which had been the setting for a quite remarkable true-life literary love story since 1961: "There was much work to be done to make it habitable again."

There remained one pleasant surprise for the new owner of
1A Ratcliffe Road. Monica instructed her solicitor that she
wanted to pay all the fees for Mr Mycock, as well as her
own. A final heart-felt gesture.
As far as I am aware, Monica was never to make contact
with anyone from Haydon Bridge again.

When I told Willie Mycock that Monica had lived for ten
years after his visit, he was amazed. "She wasn't at all well
when I was there and I thought she was on her last legs."

**In spite of her deteriorating health and solitary
existence, Monica Jones - or Miss Jones as she was
known by residents throughout her time in Haydon
Bridge - had survived Philip Larkin by fifteen years
when she passed away on 15th February 2001 in her
79th year.**

Professor James Booth describes Monica's funeral at St
Mary the Virgin, Cottingham, on 22nd February:

'The service was very Anglican; lots of mumbling to a
brightly encouraging organ, and the vicar reassuringly
informal. He was, he told us, wearing the same robes as at
Larkin's funeral. There were eighteen in the congregation.'
And at the grave side: 'It was bitterly cold and dry, with
intermittent sunshine on innumerable clumps of snowdrops.'

**Margaret Monica Beale Jones was buried on February
22nd 2001, only a few yards away from Philip Larkin,
the love of her life. Memories of Haydon Bridge laid to
rest in a Cottingham cemetery.**

Four months before his own death in 1985, Philip had
amended his will to include Monica as one of his main
beneficiaries; and Hexham Abbey was to share the benefits
accrued from this bequest, ensuring that Monica's name
lives on in Tynedale. Monica's bequest was used to fund
internal and external signage at the Abbey, and as shared
support for re-lighting of the interior and general fabric
repairs and improvements.

CHAPTER VII

MEMORIES OF MISS JONES

Haydon Bridge folk will find it remarkable that Miss Jones, the lady who lived unassumingly amongst them from 1961 to 1984, turned up as a character in a number of books and was described in 2003 by journalist Simon Hoggart as: ' … the most fictionalised real person of the last 100 years.'

Maybe you have seen Stephen Tompkinson as 'Lucky Jim' on television; or perhaps you remember the original 1957 film, the Boulting Brother's farce starring Ian Carmichael and Terry Thomas. Or maybe you have read the book published by Gollancz in 1954.
Lucky Jim was Kingsley Amis' first book and it is recognised that he owed a debt to Philip Larkin who had published *Jill*, a barely successful novel with recognisable similarities, in 1946. The two writers were close friends at Oxford and Amis dedicated his book to Philip Larkin.

Larkin made important contributions to Amis' novel, not least of which resulted in the author's portrayal of Larkin's girlfriend Monica Jones, in the character Margaret Peel, the 'unattractive' teacher obsessed with (Lucky) Jim Dixon.

The character in Amis' novel was originally named Margaret Beale - Monica's full name was Margaret Monica Beale Jones - but Larkin persuaded Amis to change Beale to Peel, in a half-hearted attempt to conceal the origin of the character when it became clear that Amis was ridiculing Monica in print. Was Kingsley Amis jealous of Monica's hold over his best friend Philip Larkin?

I can only include a brief example here of Amis' callous portrayal of Monica / Margaret. Her looks, personality and hold on Jim Dixon.

'He (Jim) could just about bring himself to praise anything but the green Paisley frock in combination with the low-heeled, quasi velvet shoes… It was a pity she wasn't better looking, that she didn't read the articles in the three-halfpenny Press that told you which colour lipstick went with which natural colouring... She always made up just a little too heavily... Her sort of minimal prettiness was in evidence... Quite soon I realised she was one of those people - they're usually women - who feed on emotional tension... Throw her a lifebelt and she'll pull you under... I'm sticking to Margaret because I haven't got the guts to turn her loose and look after herself, so I do that instead of doing what I want to do.'

If this final quote does indeed reflect Larkin's private thoughts on his relationship with Monica, as expressed to Amis, it is worth noting that when Philip and Monica were eventually brought together on a permanent basis in Hull, due to Monica's illnesses, Larkin's colleague Professor Raymond Brett points out that Philip was happy in, 'domestic contentment he had not experienced before. They were seen on Saturday mornings shopping together in Cottingham like an old married couple.'

Monica Jones has been described by those who knew her as, 'brilliantly clever'; a 'vivid and lively personality'; 'a great reader and terrific raconteur'.

As I continue my writing and research, I have in front of me a photo of a very attractive Monica in her mid-twenties. It was taken by Philip Larkin about 1947 and it is no surprise that a young man with an eye for the ladies was attracted to the glamorous and intelligent lecturer when he arrived at University College, Leicester.

Professor Watson, Monica's colleague and friend at Leicester, writes in the newsletter, '*About Larkin*' that Monica 'was a spell-binding lecturer, sweeping back her golden hair with an instinctive sense of the dramatic.'

Professor Watson continues:
'She brought colour to the place ...whoever will forget the multi-coloured hooped stockings, worn with the shortest of dresses or skirts (Monica took to the mini skirt with enthusiasm). She had a woollen dress of black and white

40

stripes, which she wore with fish-net tights.' "Newcastle United!" shouted the builders who were working on the campus: "Howay the Lads!" she would shout back.

John Ellis, a former English lecturer with Monica at Leicester is equally graphic in describing her dress sense: 'I accompanied her (to a dinner in Edinburgh University) in black tie, with Monica triumphantly wearing a purple Marks and Spencer's frilly nightdress which had taken her fancy.' "No-one will notice!" she cried, and I don't think they did.'

These memories came as no surprise to June Willis, Monica's neighbour at Haydon Bridge. June told me:

"Monica had a beautiful complexion. She was always in the fashion. Short skirts when mini skirts were popular. Big flowery-patterned dresses when flower-power was all the go." In later years at Haydon Bridge Monica's dress sense seemed to desert her but according to June: "She was never dull. One day she would wear everything white; top, dress, stockings, hat, gloves and handbag. Another day they would all be pink. Another mauve. Another all black."

It may be of course that the colours of Monica's outfits reflected her moods. This was certainly true of her when lecturing.
One of her students, Margaret Austin, remembers, 'She was always so appropriately dressed - pretty pastel shades when her topic was the Romantics; severe flowing black when she spoke of tragedy. Her hair-styles were similarly creative.'

Philip encouraged Monica to wear bright colours – her 'special clothes' - but at the same time he warned her:

'.. to the male mind, bright colours equal sexual provocation … before you know where you are the patrons of Pussy's pub* will be talking about a "hot bit who lives at the end," then they will come and try your back door. Dear be careful! ... a single lady is so defenceless.' (5th April 1966)

* *A reference to 'Merlin', the General Havelock cat Monica used to 'borrow'. (See page 44)*

There were many times when more solemn outfits were more appropriate, when a deeply upset Monica shut herself away in her Haydon Bridge cottage struggling to come to terms with Philip Larkin's other relationships - in August 1966 for example, when Larkin encouraged Maeve Brennan to write to him when he was on holiday with Monica in their secret love-nest on Ratcliffe Road.

To return to happier memories - though Monica is still dressed from head to foot in black - I am reminded of a story June Willis told me.

As a young boy, her son Tony turned the Post Office corner with his scooter just as "Miss Jones" came hurrying in the opposite direction along Church Street, from the railway station. Black hat, black dress, black-framed glasses and a black cape billowing out behind as the west wind funnelling down Ratcliffe Road caught underneath it. Tony's response to his mother was immediate. "Bloody Hell!, I've just seen Batman!"

June took some persuading to allow me to use this story, but taking into account Monica's penchant for dressing to suit the occasion and her acknowledged sense of humour, I'm sure she would have appreciated it.

June Willis was at pains to point out that Monica and Philip were, "lovely people and well-regarded by their neighbours" and she "just couldn't believe the stories about Philip and his other women," when she first heard them.

If Monica was rushing from the train around the Post Office corner, it was probably to catch the [Co-op] 'store' before it closed. She would select an easily prepared meal; maybe pre-packed sandwiches, or something in a tin. And a bottle of Moselle, her favourite wine.

It wasn't as if Monica didn't have enough tinned food set aside for a rainy day. Until Willie Mycock renovated the property the kitchen was very small and Monica's 'store' was on the stairs which led from the front door to the first floor landing. Piled-up tins of all description lined the flight of stairs. Some of the tins had been there so long that they had begun to rust. When Andrew Motion visited in 1989 the tins had leaked, 'oozing blood-coloured treacle into a puddle' at his feet. The tins of food were kept in case of emergency, not because Monica found cooking a chore. Indeed, visitors to Monica would comment upon her bread rolls and fish soup, and when June Willis was ill Monica would call in next door with a plate of her own specially prepared food for her.

Roger Craik, whose father was a colleague of Monica's at Leicester University, recalls a visit as a nine or ten year old for lunch at 'Monica's small house in Haydon Bridge': '… I had my wellington boots on and was, to my own astonishment, able to pick my way across the Tyne: it was shallow and rocky there…. But oddly (for a boy of nine or ten) it is not the paddling and the searching for trout that stick most clearly in my mind, but the soup that Monica gave us for lunch. It was a fish soup in which all manner of fishy tasty delights seemed to thrive. I think it was the first fish soup I ever had, and it had me delighting in fish soup to this day (2001). I honestly don't remember any of them being as delicious as the one Monica made.'

Haydon Bridge was, of course, a secret hideaway in many respects. Monica was very protective of her relationship with Philip and didn't court local friendships. It is no surprise, then, that I haven't met anyone, other than their neighbours, who knew the couple in the cottage on Ratcliffe Road well. Seldom is Monica's Christian name used. To most village people, the lady in 1A was "Miss Jones".

Miss Jones has been variously described to me as "a loner", "a bit arty", "hippy(ish)", "eccentric", and "a bit out of the ordinary". I am most at ease with June Willis' description: "Miss Jones was a special lady, well-educated and well - spoken but equally at home when talking to the likes of us."

Monica could arrive on the train from Leicester and be in

the house for long periods and never be seen or heard even by those next door. June would "only know Miss Jones was in residence when a grocer's van, or more likely Cato's Off-licence delivery vehicle, turned up on the doorstep."

Inside the house, with decoration and carpets that matched her sense of the dramatic - snow-white wall-to-wall in the bedroom, purple in the living room - Monica would, according to Larkin, 'retire to bed as I should sit in an armchair; surrounds herself with books and papers and seems quite comfortable.' Apparently the house was home to more books than the village library and Monica never had a television. Monica and Philip did listen to records together, however. Alan Myers reminds us that on Desert Island Discs (17th July 1976) one of Larkin's choices was 'a Newcastle street song of the 1790s 'Dollia' sung by Louis Killen'; and Johnny Handle's rendition of 'Trimdon Grange Explosion' was an inspiration to Larkin who wrote his own poem, 'The Explosion' in 1970.

Monica's love of animals was also satisfied at Ratcliffe Road. She used to 'borrow' Merlin, Mr and Mrs Clyde's Siamese cat, from the General Havelock. Monica believed it visited her for a 'bit of peace' away from the pub and it spent 'long hours on her bed'.
On one occasion, after Monica had returned to Leicester, Merlin went missing. The Clydes were distraught and a reward was posted for its safe return. June Willis continues the story:

"Lizzie Philipson was living opposite at the time. She spied the Havelock cat through Miss Jones' front room window - it must have been locked in. The Clydes were on holiday so, after feeding it for a few days with cat food through the letterbox, I rang Monica to tell her, and Philip drove her up from Hull to Haydon Bridge straightaway to let it out."

The General Havelock Inn is only a few doors along the street from 1A, and it was in this establishment where village folk recall an unseemly altercation which marred a meeting between Philip and North East poet Basil Bunting. Bunting spent the later years of his life at Whitley Chapel in Northumberland and occasionally visited the General Havelock in Haydon Bridge. During the occasion in question, it seems that Philip Larkin's unreserved right wing opinions did not sit well with Bunting's position and the two took exception to each other's political views. It is even rumoured that blows were struck during the heated discussion.

When I bought Andrew Motion's biography of Philip Larkin in 1998 and started to research the story of Monica Jones and Philip Larkin, I never imagined the extent of the Haydon Bridge connection, but the more I have written and the more I have read and enquired, the more fascinating the story has become.

Monica and Philip are no longer with us, of course, but the scene of the literary love story remains. The places they visited in and around my village; and 1A, Monica's stone built terraced cottage, the elevation fronting onto Ratcliffe Road almost unaltered.

The view of the great River Tyne, so beloved by Monica and an inspiration to Philip, continues to change daily with the weather and the seasons.

Monica's contact with Haydon Bridge ended with the sale of 1A to Willie Mycock, but Andrew Motion gives an indication that the 'Spell' was broken earlier.

In 1989, following his visit to Ratcliffe Road, he wrote:

'The house was theirs, a secret place, where she and Larkin had lived to the exclusion of all others. Dark curtained and unvisited. Once the door had been opened, that life would be over.'

The quarter share of £1 million bequeathed to Hexham Abbey is an indication that Miss Jones' love affair with Tynedale lingered until the day she died; and the literary legacy of **1A, Ratcliffe Road** writes another chapter in the colourful history of Haydon Bridge and its Parish.

REQUIESCAT

She is all quiet now, only the sea
Booms sadly, sighing, surging over the hill,
And a bird in the trees is singing, singing, - but she
Who was herself once like a bird, is still.

Nothing will break her quiet, here where she sleeps
Only the wild birds circle over her.
She will not know the dawn, or when night creeps
Cold-fingered, lays sleep on the flowers that cover her.

She is gone from us now, she is sleeping
Here, where there is no weariness, only repose;
For her there is no more anger, or sorrow, or weeping;
If she is forgot or remembered, she cares not, nor knows.

Rest she has found; and she has been very tired,
And now she has done with the world's turmoil and care;
Doubtless one might find a peace here, and peace she
desired,
Now the quiet old earth is over her eyes and her hair.

*Written by Monica Jones and published in the
Kidderminster Girls' High School Magazine in 1938
and in the 'About Larkin' newsletter in October 2001*

**Philip and Monica are buried a few yards apart
in Cottingham Cemetery.
(photographs by Graham and Susan Beales)**

Monica's interment at Cottingham Cemetery. © James Booth

(Monica's) funeral was a moving occasion, even though the congregation was very small; Monica would have approved of it. The vicar very properly used the Book of Common Prayer service, and read Psalm 39: 'Behold, thou hast made my days as it were a span long: and mine age is even as nothing I respect of thee; and verily every man living is altogether vanity.' She would have loved the old words, and the quiet dignity of it; and also the final hymn (perhaps she had left word that she wanted it sung). As we sang 'The day thou gavest, Lord is ended', I remembered her telling me once of a time when, on the way back from holiday somewhere, she sang it to Philip verse by verse:

J.R. Watson 'About Larkin' No 11 April 2001

Philip Arthur Larkin.
Born: 9th August 1922
Died: 2nd December 1985

Margaret Monica Beale Jones
Born: 7th May 1922
Died: 15th February 2001

**Hexham Abbey, an historic place of worship
to which Monica bequeathed part of her legacy.**

**Just under £1 million from Monica's will was shared equally
between Hexham Abbey, Durham Cathedral,
St Paul's Cathedral and the National Trust.**

APPENDIX 1

A SELECTION OF EXTRACTS FROM LETTERS BETWEEN PHILIP AND MONICA, RELATING TO HAYDON BRIDGE

Selected by Anthony Thwaite
for
'Philip Larkin - Letters to Monica'
First published by Faber and Faber Ltd 2010

Selected and edited for this publication by the author

Thanks also to June Willis and the Willis family for the letter on page 57
and
The Society of Authors
Literary Representatives of the Estate of Philip Larkin

First published by Faber and Faber Ltd 2010
'Philip Larkin - Letters to Monica' by Anthony Thwaite

Letters are from Philip to Monica unless otherwise stated

17 August 1961
Pearson Park, Hull

Dearest,
   ... And as regards Hexham, are you going up with the luggage next
week?

*Note: Monica had just bought her cottage, 1A Ratcliffe Road, in Haydon
Bridge.*

---

2 October 1961
   32 Pearson Park, Hull

... I'm less jealous of the cat. I hope its owners don't turn it out on the
assumption that it has a new home. Is it a nice cat? I forget what colour
you said it was. ...

*Note: Monica used to 'borrow' Merlin, Mr and Mrs Clyde's cat, from the
General Havelock.*

11 April 1962
   32 Pearson Park, Hull

... I thought your little house seemed (how fond I seem of that
word!) distinguished and exciting and beautiful: clever of you to
have found it, bold of you to have furnished it in Rabbit Regency: it
looks splendid, and it can never be ordinary with the Tyne going by
outside. Others may have Swedish glass, or Swedish forks, or
Finnish clap-boarding, or theatre in the round round the corner, or a
Picasso, or a stereo hi-fi, or a split-level living area - *you* have a
great English river drifting under your window, brown and muscled
with currents!

Note: Philip's response following his first visit to Haydon Bridge.

26/27 September 1962 *(Letter from Monica)*
Haydon Bridge

… You know how you are often trying to talk to me about us, & I always start to cry so you can't; I wish I didn't, but it just makes me cry to think of it, so I try not to think of it - all the same, I'm sorry, because I think you ought to be able to say something without tears from me, & indeed I wish I could talk about it without tears. Nevertheless I do think abt it sometimes, and today is a day that has made me think of it - the summer going, unused, the beauty of the scenery, unused. It made me very conscious of what a short time we are here for & how little of that time we have left, you and I; it isn't much, and for all we know it might be very short, & I wish I could spend what is left with you, or more of what is left than I do spend. I can write this, just, but I'm sure I couldn't say it - I am not in tears, but tears are behind my eyes, making eyes & head ache. If once I start thinking of reality, *all* the sad things lock to mind at once, & all the impossible difficulty of life, the way I just scrape along, never, never being in control of the situation, never doing anything properly, & I can hardly bear it. I live so foolishly, too; wasting hours in lazy inertia, doing *nothing*, or thinking sadly and pointlessly, always worried abt things undone & my inability to get on with them; and I do rely on drink more than I like, I really have to have my tipple, now, & *sometimes* I drink a lot, tho' not, I think, as badly now as I did just after my parents died.

———

29 September 1962
32 Pearson Park, Hull

Well, of course, I do understand and agree with what you say, when you say how we are wasting our lives. When I say I wish we could talk more easily about ourselves, I mean just that; I mean it seems strange not to, and I think it's something of a barrier between us, or a failure between us - it's difficult to know precisely what I mean: …

I can't say how badly I feel about the way we are wasting our lives: it terrifies me, and gets worse every day. …

Sunday …

My dear, I don't think you are incompetent, or whatever you said you were in your letter: I think you are very good at knowing what should be done, very good at not being afraid of doing it, and pretty good at doing it. Big things, I mean. In little day to day things I don't know - you seem to *drag* rather, represented by your unwillingness to have the right time anywhere about, ...

———

1 October 1962 *(Letter from Monica)*
Haydon Bridge

I wish I were better - I'd like to be able to talk more. I think I could have, when we began, perhaps; but I never know what you are thinking, and thinking of me - and you must admit, with some reason, you *have* been attracted to various people and haven't told me. I don't think I'm too much to be blamed for being so tiresome - I do not behave reasonably, I know, & I wish I did; but it is not an *easy* situation, as you know & wish to say, I suppose, & I think it can be understood that I am very easily upset abt it ... Anyway, I accept, don't I, & *without* private reservation or grudge, that you don't like me enough to marry me; then it seems rather unkind for you to want to *tell* me so, & perhaps tell me all the things that are wrong with me.

---

4 October 1962
32 Pearson Park, Hull

Dearest,
  You must think me awful, as if I deliberately set out to upset you - I'm sorry: it isn't that. I am *always* oppressed by guilt-feelings about the mess I have got you in, and my own behaviour seems so bad anyway that almost anything else wd seem better, in the way of behaviour I mean. ...
  You know, I expect you do want to feel reassured, but I always fall into the habit of thinking you are more assured than I am: you have such a strong, seamless character - not vague, shifting and gullible like mine - and you have a - really, I wd swear it - stronger personality than mine: you aren't given to bursts of temper or vindictiveness but are much more level and firm than I. For this reason I am always feeling I deserve a denunciation from you - I always feel morally inferior, not only relatively in the way I have behaved but absolutely in comparing ourselves. And of course I do feel terrible about our being 40 & unmarried. I fear we are to turn slowly into living reproaches of the way I have dallied and lingered with you, neither one thing or the other. This leads me to spells of wanting to explain & defend myself, wch appears like brutal & gratuitous attack to you, but wch are really products of miserable self accusation - ... And then again I hope if only we could achieve, I don't know, a kind of self-encouraging intimacy, it wd be so easy for us to marry. But this may be fancy on my part - people are different, after all.

August 1965
21 York Road Loughborough

Dearest Bun,
  Yes, that Abbey shop is fine. I went to it at least twice but it was always closed. I don't know that I wanted anything, but I should have liked to look round. How kind of you to send me the Newcastle songs! Mother is highly amused at the sack of sawdust concept. The laylock nightgown is very appropriate too. *(Note: References relate to Geordie Ridley's 'Cushie Butterfield'.)* I wish I could read the tunes: I like such of them as I know. We used to sing the *Keel Row* at school, so that's well rubbed in.

Note:
Monica retained a number of artefacts in Hull until the day she died, as a reminder of Northumberland and her liaison with Philip at 1A, Ratcliffe Road, Haydon Bridge. The artefacts are part of the Larkin archive at Hull University and include four 12" Long Playing Records, and the EP from which Philip chose his second record of 'Dollia' on Desert Island Discs.
Northumberland For Ever: *Dance & Song from The High Level Ranters.*
Holey Ha'penny: *Classic recordings of traditional music from the North East of England, including Haydon Bridge's Jimmy Hunter on harmonica.*
Along The Coaly Tyne: *Songs of the North East of England by Johnny Handle, Louis Killen, Tom Gilfellon, Colin Ross and Alastair Anderson.*
Songs of the North East and the Borders: *E.P. Louis Killen and Colin Ross.*

All the above are on the Topic label

Blaydon Races: *Michael Hunt and the Dombie Brothers. (Eclipse label)*

A record sleeve of 'The Unique Night Stars', with Hexham Abbey on the cover, was also recovered from the house at Hull.

---

12 November 1967
  32 Pearson Park, Hull

… I enclose 3 more Bellingham pictures. I love the one of the wrestlers - it absolutely has the scene as it was, the odd ritualistic stance & garb of the wrestlers, & the rural crowd in a circle. What a lovely day it was! It will stay in my mind for ever, it was lovely.

Note: This is the scene that evoked in Larkin's poem 'Show Saturday' - completed 3rd December 1973.

54

4 August 1968
Pearson Park, Hull

Dearest Bun,
… Your village certainly sounds full of action: frightening, almost. Like
The Devil At Saxon Wall. Mrs Passion and Mrs Fluke. Well, not quite,
with the main road from Newcastle to Carlisle running under the
windows, …
Yes, do keep your short hair. It makes you look lighter & younger &
gayer: I like it very much. I wish I could find something to do the same
for me.

_____

12 October 1982
105 Newland Park, Hull

Dearest Bun,
… Am naturally *very* worried about your face & wound. Do get the
doctor: think of all you've paid in tax for him. This is the sort of thing he
can treat. Think of *boxers* - the are v. worried abt eyebrows. …
Darling, I am so worried about you. Why not ask Mrs Willis to help?
You could ring her, & leave door open. We shall talk before you get this.
Rest, but eat, and *tell doctor.* All love Philip

Note: Monica had fallen down the stairs at 1A Ratcliffe Road.

_____

13 October 1982
105 Newland Park, Hull

Dearest Bun,
The hospital rang up at nearly six today, so I knew you were safe, but oh
dear, how nastily you must have been hurt, and what pain and distress it
must have caused, *Poor Bun!* And what a shock to be swept out of daily
life into Hexham General Hospital. I rang them tonight about 8. The line,
Geordie accent & my deafness made it difficult, but I gathered I might
have spoken to you if something or other. As it was, I sent love. I will
come & see you on Sunday (2 - 4) … The nurse said they expected you
would be in 'over the weekend', but no doubt stitches take some time to
heal. And you will be looked after, wch will save trouble. But I am
awfully sorry that such trouble should befall you. Those stairs are a

55

menace. I have to come down them like a pregnant giraffe.

I remember Hexham General is good for something, so hope it is good for everything. What is the food like? Are you 'allowed up'? Can you hear the Archers? Or is it all telly? I do hope you can rest, and get a night's sleep.

I sent you a card-in-envelope to HB, but it will be waiting there. ...

Dear Bun, I know how utterly alien hospitals are, but I hope this one is kind and friendly, and that you don't feel too shaken. Can you get a paper? And a pencil for the crossword? Think if you would like to come here to convalesce when you 'come out'. I could fetch you away. ...

My dear, I think of you all the time, but will *see you* on Sunday. Much, much love. Philip

---

14 October 1982
105 Newland Park, Hull

Dearest Bun,

Oh dear, I am not one of nature's hospital-telephoners. Having finally got Ward 11 tonight, I couldn't hear a word they said. 'Was I a relative?' No - well, gibber-gibber-gibber gibber gibber. I tried to explain that I was intending to come up on Sunday if you were still resident, but gibber gibber. I tried to send love. In consequence I don't know how you are, or what wd have happened if I *had* been a relative. Feel worried and cross with myself. I should *say* I am deaf.

How wonderful it will be to talk to you again! It seems an age since we spoke. Are you finding it bearable? do you miss drinks? I *do* hope you are all right, and not made ill by being in hospital. I expect it is very boring - that is the best it can be. Let it be no worse.

How are you finding the food? Perhaps that could be the worst. ...

I do wonder how you are. Did you bring anything to read? Was it all very rushed, having to snatch up a few necessaries? Poor Bun, I do feel for you. I wonder if you are all bound up over the stitches, and how long will it take. Are you allowed to walk about? It's so hard for me to imagine. ... Unless I hear anything different I shall set out on Sunday morning after breakfast & hope to fall in when they open the doors at 2 pm. Have nothing to bring, unless you'd like *The Doctor's Dilemma*. Very much love, dear bun.

Philip

---

105 Newland Park
Hull

Dear June,

Thank you very much for letting me know about the storm damage - I was not too surprised, as the weather report sounded rather alarming.

Yes please do ask Mr Charlton to do what repairs he thinks necessary to my house as soon as he can.

Since I saw you Philip has had 'flu and then a spell of phlebitis in his leg, he is now back to work after three weeks off, and his consultant appears quite pleased with his progress; & we hope all you are well. I had thought I would be back in Haydon Bridge before now, but had to stay here until this bad patch was over.

Thank you again for letting me know about the roof, & for keeping an eye on my house generally. I hope all goes well with you & the family.

All good wishes

Monica Jones

A letter from Monica to June Willis, her neighbour at Haydon Bridge.

Author's Note!

Philip was off work with phlebitis in February 1984. It follows that this letter was probably written in March 1984

57

2 April 1984
   105 Newland Park, Hull

Tues.

Dearest Bun,
   Monday evening - safely back. Went Tow Law way, & at Scotch Corner
(stopped for a piss), continued down motorway, ... House 54° - regular
greenhouse after Lord Crewe.
   Of course I have thought of you constantly, wondering how you are
feeling and doing. Did you have your bath? I hope you did and feel more
restored and relaxed. Indeed I can't imagine you'll be any less *feeble* but
I hope you find some satisfaction in being among your own things, and
your own boss again. Be careful, dear, of *stairs & road crossings*, and be
sensible about eating & drinking.
   Dear Bun, thank you for your company and all your kindnesses. You are
courageous and patient. Hope you are finding it possible to manage.

Much love
Philip

*Note: Following a diagnosis of shingles in March 1983, Monica had
returned to Hull where she spent a year with Philip. In late March 1984,
she hoped to be sufficiently recovered to look after herself and Philip had
driven her back to Haydon Bridge.*

----

3 April 1984
   105 Newland Park, Hull

... Of course I have missed you, ... found myself putting the butter out for
you for breakfast! I do hope you have felt a little more at home and able
to do things. I look forward to hearing what you feel like: it's awful being
cut off like this, quite the last straw. ...

*Note: Within a few days - when the telephone was reconnected - Monica
rang Philip and he happily took her back from Haydon Bridge to Hull
where they lived together at 105 Newland Park.
This was to be their last visit to **1A, Ratcliffe Road in Haydon Bridge**.*

APPENDIX 2

BREAKING IN
BY
ANDREW MOTION

Following his visit to 1A, Ratcliffe Road in 1989
First published in GRANTA Magazine in 1992

EXTRACTS FROM 'BREAKING IN' by ANDREW MOTION

In June 1983, when (Monica) was sixty-one, recently retired from Leicester, and living in Haydon Bridge more or less full-time, she developed shingles. Larkin, who was staying, took charge. He ferried her south to Hull and put her in hospital, where she lay half-blinded and in great pain for several days. Then he brought her back to his own house in Hull. She stayed ten months - until the following April - before returning to Haydon Bridge, meaning to re-start her independent life. But she was still unwell, and anyway Larkin missed her. Within a few days he had decided to collect her again. He helped her pack, then sat in the car while she checked for last things, drew the curtains, switched off the electricity at the meter, and locked the front door. Anxiously, he drove her back to Hull.

Larkin thought Monica was fatally ill. In fact, he was. Within a year he was in hospital for tests; on 2 December 1985 he died of cancer. Monica stayed in Hull - depressed, sick and exhausted. She wanted her own life back but couldn't reach it. She worried about her house in Haydon Bridge but was too ill to get herself there.

Early in 1986 Monica asked me to write Larkin's biography, and over the next few years we saw a great deal of each other. She sat in what had once been Larkin's chair, his tweed coat still slung over the arm. I sat on the sofa, his Rowlandson watercolour on the dark green wall behind me. Sometimes I formally interviewed her; sometimes we just chatted. Sometimes we looked at photographs of him or by him; sometimes we read his books. There was no hurry. She had known Larkin better than anyone. I had to ransack her memory.

Monica said nothing about the letters Larkin had written her. If I asked where they were she would shrug - lighting another cigarette, pouring another drink. Did this mean she didn't want me to see them? Or had they, like his diaries, been destroyed? She wasn't telling.

One day out of the blue she said most of the letters were in Haydon Bridge. Why didn't we drive up together to get them? It was a forlorn hope - she was too ill - yet she didn't want me to go without her. The house was theirs: a secret place, where she and Larkin had lived to the exclusion of all others. Dark-curtained and unvisited, it held their continuing, unbroken life together.

Once the door had been opened, that life would be over.

Months passed. Monica grew more frail. Eventually she decided I would have to go alone. I drove up with a friend from Hull, Marion Shaw, in the autumn of 1989. As far as I knew, no one had been into the house for five years.

We roller-coastered the wet road towards Hexham, then on. Rain was swirling in from the North Sea behind us. So much had fallen in recent weeks, the moors were yellow and sour-looking. As we ducked down into Haydon Bridge, streams bulged in the ditches beside us. The house was even smaller than I'd expected, and uglier. Packed into a tight row near the Old Bridge, on the main road, it had a jaded white front, a slate roof, plain modern windows and a front door which opened straight off the street. I got the key from a neighbour and opened up - but the door was stuck. Peering through the letter-box, the rain falling on my neck and back, I could see why. There was a mound of junk mail on the mat: offers of free film, estate agents' bumf, cards from taxi companies and window cleaners.

I shoved the door violently and we were in. A tiny box of a hall; the sitting-room to the left; stairs rising straight ahead. The stairs looked crazy. There was no carpet (just the pale section where a carpet had once been) and at the sides of each step - cans of food. One of these had leaked, oozing blood-coloured treacle into a puddle at my feet, I tried to wipe it up, scrape it up, somehow get rid of it, with a piece of junk mail. It was impossible. In the end I hid it beneath a few bright envelopes.

The smell was worse when I turned on the electricity. Sweet open-air dampness like a rotten log - but also fusty. And there was noise too, noise I couldn't recognize. A roaring, but some-how subdued. When I turned into the sitting-room I understood. Outside the window at the back, beyond a cramped cement yard and a tow-path, there flowed a gigantic river. The Tyne; invisible from the road. Within the first few seconds of looking, I saw a full-grown tree sweep past, then heard the trunk grinding against the bridge away to my left, out of sight.

The window was broken - a hole like a star-burst and slivers of glass on the purple carpet.

We weren't the first people here for years, we were the second and third - at least the second and third. The drawers in a side-board lolled open, empty; in the grate, jagged pieces of crockery poked out of a sootfall; there was a dark circle in the dust on a table where a vase had stood. And there were books all over the floor - books flung about for the hell of it - and a deep scar on the window-seat where something heavy had been manhandled into the yard then away along the towpath.

We tiptoed through the shambles, closing up, straightening, tidying, our hands immediately grey with dust. It was wet dust, sticking to us and clinging in our noses and lungs. Monica hadn't told me where I might find the letters, but it didn't matter. They were everywhere. In books, down the side of a chair, under a rug, on the window-seat. A few lay flat and saturated in the yard, scrabbled out when the last burglar left.

It was the same upstairs, though the dust seemed lighter there, maybe because the rain had eased off outside and the sun was starting to break through. The river sounded quieter, too, and I could see a family on the opposite bank - a man, a woman and two children, walking a dog.

I went into the lumber room, into a jungle of clothes and hangers which had a small box at its heart, stuffed with letters.

Nothing in the bathroom.

In the smaller bedroom: under the window overlooking the river, a bed with letters both inside and underneath it, and a cupboard crowded with damp dresses which tore when I touched them.

In the larger bedroom: more letters in books, an empty case of wine, an ironing board with a half-ironed dress draped across it.

When I got downstairs I realized I was breathing in gulps, as if I were swimming.

We counted the letters into plastic bags. There were nearly two hundred of them. Then we went through the house again, found the last handful, turned off the electricity, locked up, returned the key to the neighbour, arranged for the window to be repaired and climbed into the car. The sun had gone in; it was starting to rain again. Larkin had sat in the same place, squinnying at the little house, feeling anxious. I felt exhilarated and ashamed.

I wasn't the last. A week or so after I'd taken the letters back to Monica, a van drew up outside the house in Haydon Bridge and two people got out, kicked open the front door and stole nearly everything inside. If the letters had still been there, they would have gone too. By the time this happened, I'd read them - and two hundred or so more, that Monica revealed Larkin had written to her in Leicester. _____

AFTERWORD

Tune: Rothbury Hills (Jack Armstrong)

Now you can decide whether these lines of mine,
Tell a story that's happy of a love that's sublime;
Or maybe it's sad, when her love was away with
Another he loved just as well.

But one day she was sure he would back to her come,
To the banks of the Tyne where the best salmon run;
In a little stone cottage, he'd forget for a day
Another he loved just as well.

There he'd swear that he never would leave her again,
And that they both together would ever remain;
Make a promise, not ever once more would he stray to
Another he loved just as well.

———————

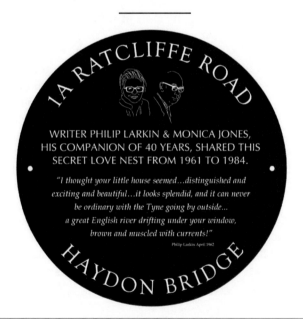

1A RATCLIFFE ROAD

WRITER PHILIP LARKIN & MONICA JONES,
HIS COMPANION OF 40 YEARS, SHARED THIS
SECRET LOVE NEST FROM 1961 TO 1984.

*"I thought your little house seemed…distinguished and
exciting and beautiful…it looks splendid, and it can never
be ordinary with the Tyne going by outside…
a great English river drifting under your window,
brown and muscled with currents!"*

Philip Larkin April 1962

HAYDON BRIDGE

Thanks are due to Haydon Parish Council; to parish clerk Carole McGivern, for her help in securing permissions; to Marcus Byron for the preparation of the plaque on 1A; and to Jeannie and Bill Lally, the owners of 1A in 2014.